True Tales
OF BIRMINGHAM

A Series of Weekly Columns
which originally appeared
from February, 1991 to April, 1992
in *The Birmingham News.*

Larry Ragan

Published by
Birmingham Historical Society

Cover illustrations:
Top left to right, Robert Jemison, Jr., Vincent and Theresa Bruno,
Carrie Tuggle, statue of Vulcan; bottom left to right, Erskine Ramsey,
John ("Brother") Bryan, Thomas Tennessee Hillman.

For information on membership or to purchase additional copies
of TRUE TALES or other Society publications, please contact the
Society's offices at Duncan House located on the grounds of Sloss
Furnaces National Historical Landmark.
One Sloss Quarters, Birmingham, Alabama 35222
Telephone: 205-251-1880 • www.bhistorical.org

Library of Congress Catalog Number: 92-08271
ISBN Number: 0-943994-19-5

Printed in Canada

Preface

This book is a collection of columns published in The Birmingham News. A project of the Birmingham Historical Society, True Tales first appeared in the Comics section of the News every Saturday from February, 1991 through April, 1992.

Why mix history and comic strips? Because people of all ages and backgrounds enjoy the funny pages. It was our goal to show the reader that history is not a static record of the past. It is a vital pulse in all our lives, one that can help prepare us and our children for future challenges.

Even as an infant community, Birmingham had plenty of positive role models. These men and women, both young and old, met life's hardships head on and worked to lessen them for others. For example:

* She left her rural home at an early age and moved to the Magic City. On its streets she soon became the champion of homeless boys ... standing by them in court and finally founding a school for them.

* Disabled at age seven, he spent six years learning about rehabilitation. After becoming a successful businessman, he used his wealth to help others who were sick become well again.

This publication contains profiles of remarkable people and the places associated with them. These individuals helped change an industrial boom town of the 1880s into a modern city with a rich cultural heritage. In these pages, the issues of racial, social and religious differences become secondary to portraits of courage and compassion and a willingness to take risks and pursue ambitious goals. This book is dedicated not only to the great people in it, but to the thousands who made their unsung contributions to Birmingham's growth as the Magic City, the industrial capital of the South.

Larry Ragan

Table of Contents

Railroad Engineer & City Planner

While John Milner was still a teenager, his father did extensive railroad contracting in Georgia. Young Milner worked at all aspects of building railroads and also tried his hand at gold mining. In 1842, he decided to strike out on his own.

Milner drove a team of oxen across the plains to Oregon and California. There, his hands-on experience in construction served him well, and he was appointed City Surveyor of San Jose, then the capital of the state.

After 10 years, he returned to Georgia and soon afterward came to Alabama. In 1858, he was selected chief engineer for South & North Alabama Railroad, the state-sponsored railroad intended to link the port city of Mobile to Montgomery and Nashville and to open development of the state's mineral resources. Milner became the railroad's chief advocate and promoter as well as its routing engineer.

Milner was one of the first to envision a great industrial city in northern Alabama. In the 1870s, his expertise in railroad routing led him to choose the site for his "ideal" city. His choice — in Jones Valley at the juncture of two major railroad lines — became the setting for the new city of Birmingham. When his railroad (later a part of the L. & N. and now CSX system) arrived, the city boomed.

Milner then turned his attention to the area's wealth of mineral resources.

John T. Milner (1826-1898)

He went into coal mining and eventually became a state senator. As a politician, he continued working to develop industry in Alabama.

The building of railroad lines and industrial plants made Birmingham a city that grew like magic. By the turn of the century, Birmingham had become the rail capital of the South. Freight trains, like this one pictured in 1910 near today's Century Plaza, hauled large tonnages of coal, cast-iron pipe and steel.

From Slave to Inventor

Andrew J. Beard (1849-1921)

Born a slave on a plantation near Mt. Pinson, Andrew Jackson Beard had no formal education. He learned instead how to care for animals, make plants grow, and fix things when they broke. Because he was gifted with imagination and intelligence, young Andrew excelled at all these tasks, especially the last.

As a grown man working for the railroad, Beard created gadgets that solved on-the-job problems. His experiments soon led to an idea that was worth protecting with a patent. Since Beard could not read or write, he turned to Birmingham's mayor, Melville Drennen.

With Drennen's help, Beard completed the necessary forms, and on July 5, 1892, he was granted a patent on a rotary engine. When he later saw a man lose an arm while trying to couple two rail cars together, he went to work on his most famous and profitable invention, the automatic car-coupling device.

This invention not only saved lives and limbs of railroad workers around the world, it also made Beard a rich man; he is thought to be Jefferson County's first black millionaire.

This 1883 photograph shows a Georgia Pacific switch engine. Andrew Jackson Beard's fascination with these trains led to the invention that saved many lives and made him a rich man.

Pony Express Rider & Promoter

James R. Powell (1814-1873)

Tall, lanky, outspoken James Powell was 19 years old when he gave up his teaching job in Virginia and headed south in 1833. When he reached Montgomery a few months later, all Powell had to his name was $20, a bag of salt and meal, and his horse.

Powell had to sell his horse before finally landing a job as a mail rider for the pony express. At that time, express riders were heroes of the road. Men, women, and children often ran outside to watch Powell thunder through on the Nashville to Montgomery run.

When the express was abolished, he started his own mail and passenger coach operation, building it into a multi-state empire. Powell also invested in cotton lands. Just 12 years after selling his horse to survive, he was elected to the state legislature.

Always forward-looking, Powell saw the great potential of Jones Valley for industrial development. In 1870, joining other southern entrepreneurs, he established the company that founded Birmingham. He became its first president and most energetic promoter. Powell personally supervised the laying out of the streets and lots in a swampy, overgrown cornfield, convincing purchasers and investors that a great industrial center would soon arise. Citizens responded by electing him as their first mayor.

As mayor, Powell donated his salary for use in establishing the city's first school.

Birmingham's first school is named for James R. Powell. At the time of its construction (1887), Powell School, still located at Sixth Avenue North and 24th Street, was considered the most modern and best equipped in the South.

Banker & Builder

At the age of 15, Maryland-born Josiah Morris abandoned the idea of going to college and set out alone for the south. He settled first in Georgia and, with the help of a local judge, started a career in finance.

Sixteen years later Morris moved to New Orleans and, after a short stay there, moved to Montgomery

This 1910 photograph shows Morris Avenue, the city's earliest wholesale district. In 1973, it became the city's first National Register Historic District. Today, lawyers, architects, loft residents and artists occupy the attractively renovated brick warehouses.

Josiah Morris (1818-1891)

where he established his own private bank. Recognizing the important role that railroads would play in the development of the state, Morris served as director of two statewide railroad companies.

After the Civil War, several entrepreneurs decided that Jones Valley would be the ideal site for a new city since two of the state's major rail lines would cross there. Morris became involved in the city's development.

On Dec. 19, 1870, Morris paid $100,000 in cash for 4,150 acres of land at the proposed crossing. The next day, he and other southern investors formed a company (the Elyton Land, later Birmingham Realty Co.) to build a city there. Because coal and iron ore resources in the area gave promise that the city would become a manufacturing center, Morris named it Birmingham after Birmingham, England, then the world's largest industrial center.

Blockade Runner & Banker

Charles Linn was born Carl Eric Englebert Schodal in a coastal village of Finland to Swedish parents. In 1829, at the age of 15, he went to sea as a cabin boy. During the next four years he made 65 trips across the Atlantic and finally decided to stay in America when his boat docked in New York in 1833.

With no friends and no job, Linn bought a supply of tinware, strapped it to his back, and worked his way south peddling these goods. In Montgomery, he became partner in a fruit stand that quickly grew into a bakery and wholesale grocery. In 1842, he returned to Europe to marry his childhood sweetheart. Upon their return, he changed his name to Charles Linn since he believed his given name was too hard for Americans to pronounce.

Linn's Montgomery-based business venture continued to grow, but tragedy struck the family when his wife died in 1852. With the outbreak of the Civil War in 1861, he sent his second wife and family to Germany and used his ship "Kate Dale" as a blockade runner.

Charles Linn (1814-1883)

Linn and his son were captured in 1865 but were pardoned when the war ended.

In 1872, James Powell, President of the Elyton Land Company, lured Linn to Birmingham to establish the city's first bank. Many said the city was too young to need a bank, but Linn's "First National Bank," the forerunner of today's AmSouth Bank, flourished as did the iron works and the city in which he invested.

Linn expressed a desire to be buried on a high knoll in Oak Hill Cemetery, so that on Judgment Day, he could walk out and see the "greatest industrial city in the South."

Educator & Historian

*Isaac Wellington McAdory
(1843-1922)*

Isaac McAdory was born in 1843 in the rural farming community of Pleasant Hill in western Jefferson County. Educated at the Jonesboro Salem Academy, he joined the Confederate Army in 1862.

McAdory served in the Army of Tennessee from the time of the Battle of Shiloh until 1865 when Gen. Joseph E. Johnston surrendered his forces in North Carolina. During that time, he kept notebooks and diaries that provide valuable insight and information about the daily trials of a common soldier during those times.

In 1866, he began teaching in Pleasant Hill and taught 11 months a year for the next 23 years. In 1874, he married Alice Sadler, whose family had also been pioneer settlers of eastern Jefferson County. She was a graduate of the Tuscaloosa Female College and a fellow teacher at Pleasant Hill.

McAdory became county superintendent of education in 1899 and remained at that post until 1913. During that time public schools were established within reach of children in all communities of the county. McAdory also served two terms in the state legislature. Today, McAdory School in McCalla is named for this dedicated educator.

The Sadler and McAdory Houses, built in the mid-19th century as self-sufficient rural plantations, remain today along Eastern Valley Road near Bessemer. Pictured here is the Sadler House.

Pioneer Healthcare Leader

Mortimer Jordan was born in Jefferson County in 1844. During his childhood, he worked on his father's farm and attended local schools.

After spending two years at the University of Alabama, he enlisted as a private in the Confederate Army. Jordan rose to the rank of captain by the end of the war. Afterwards, he decided to study medicine in the office of his uncle.

In the spring of 1867, he graduated at the head of his class from Miami Medical College in Cincinnati, Ohio. Dr. Jordan then returned to Elyton (at that time the county seat of Jefferson County) and began to practice medicine.

Two years later, he was appointed to the physician's post at the Alabama State Penitentiary in Wetumpka. During his term there, he discovered a prevalence of scurvy

Mortimer H. Jordan (1844-1889)

among the convicts and corrected it with a change of diet.

In 1873, he moved to the then infant city of Birmingham. That same year, a major cholera epidemic struck the new community and Dr. Jordan worked night and day to keep it under control. Thanks, in major part, to his tireless efforts, the Magic City survived and flourished. Dr. Jordan's practice flourished also, and he became a leader in the delivery of the city's health care. The administration building at the University of Alabama at Birmingham is named in his honor.

Bethlehem Methodist Church at Rutledge Springs, just west of the USX Fairfield Works and just east of the former Jordan farm site, is one of Birmingham's earliest religious structures. Logs from the 1818 church still remain within the turn-of-the-century clapboard church. Jordan and other pioneer farmers are buried in the nearby graveyard.

Founding Spirit

Annie Linn was born in Montgomery in 1849. When the Civil War began, her wealthy family sent her to Europe to continue her education.

In 1872, the Linn family moved to the new city of Birmingham. At that time, Birmingham was a frontier community filled with "poor and rough" citizens, mostly men.

Annie Linn was determined to help bring culture to the town she grew to love. She helped found the first literary club (the Cadmean Circle, now 104 years old), taught Sunday school, and was instrumental in establishing Birmingham's first major hospital (the Hillman Hospital).

She married Capt. John Henley in 1876. Through the years, they had three sons, and although Annie added rearing a family to her busy schedule, she always found time to promote the Magic City.

At the turn of the century, railroads were the main means of travel. Annie Linn often met the incoming trains, greeted the passengers who were stopping in Birmingham, and did her best to help them settle.

Throughout her life, Annie Linn Henley was instrumental in shaping the cultural, intellectual, business and religious development of her beloved city.

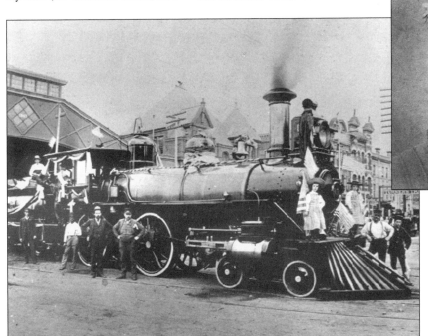

Annie Linn Henley (1849-1929)

Annie Linn Henley met incoming trains at the old Union Station (to the left in this 1890 photograph), welcoming new arrivals to the booming industrial city.

Alabama's First Industrialist

Daniel Pratt (1799-1873)

Daniel Pratt began his career as a carpenter's apprentice. The New England native spent four years learning the carpentry trade. Pratt then headed south, arriving in Savannah, Ga., with his chest of tools and his builder's skills. He spent the next 14 years working from "can to can't" in various locations in the state.

In 1833, at age 34, Pratt moved to Alabama in order to manufacture cotton gins. His success in this venture was considerable, and he eventually founded a model industrial community around his booming business.

He selected a site in the piney woods and marshes just north of Montgomery. His intent was utopian: "to build a village dignifying labor in the South." His village, Prattville, became the county seat and industrial center of the state. Its founder also served in the state legislature.

By the early 1870s, Pratt's interests turned to railroads and the development of mineral resources in the Birmingham area. Pratt's fortune financed vast developments in the new industrial city. The area's principal coal seam and mining town were named in his honor.

In 1884, Birmingham entrepreneurs sent this ll-ton lump of Pratt coal to the New Orleans World Exposition. It ignited international interest in the area's mineral resources.

The Treasure of Red Mountain

Baylis Earle Grace (1808-1893)

Long before white settlers came to Alabama, the "long hill of dye-rock" was well known to the natives of this region. Throughout the 1800s, pioneers used this reddish stone, which was actually iron ore, to dye woolen and cotton fabrics. At this time, a few bars of iron were priceless and several area black-smiths tried, without success, to forge iron from the mountain's rich supply of reddish ore.

In 1820, 12-year-old Baylis Grace came to Jefferson County with his parents. Later orphaned, he served under prominent citizens at the settlement of Elyton and eventually became sheriff of the county and editor of the area's earliest newspaper. But it was his interest in the red "dye-rock" of Red Mountain that led to his biggest contribution to the area.

Convinced that the mountain's ore could be turned into good iron, Grace bought a farm along the crest of the mountain at a site just north of Oxmoor and still known as Grace's Gap. In the 1850s, he sent a wagon load of ore from his land here to a puddling furnace in Bibb County where it was successfully turned into iron. For the rest of his life, Grace kept one of those iron bars on his desk as a prized exhibit — one that reminded him that a good idea is worth pursuing no matter what others think.

From the Civil War through the 1960s, Red Mountain provided iron ore to fire furnaces in the Birmingham industrial district.

From Forge to Furnace

Ninion Tannehill, a Jefferson County cotton planter and stock breeder, invested in the construction of the earliest iron furnace at Tannehill.

In the fall of 1830, several local planters decided to experiment with iron manufacture. Enlisting the aid of Daniel Hillman, a seasoned ironmaster from New Jersey, they built a water-powered forge on the banks of Roupes Creek which provided plows, horseshoes and hollow-ware for the farming community.

Hillman's Forge underwent a major expansion in the late 1850s when Moses Stroup built the first blast furnace on the site. With financing from the Confederate government, W. L. Sanders added two more stone furnaces in 1862, making the Tannehill ironworks the only site in the state with three furnaces side by side.

The furnaces, with a 20 ton daily output, supplied iron to the Selma Arsenal for the manufacture of cannon and naval plate. This made them an important target for Union forces which stormed the state in the spring of 1865.

Just nine days before Lee surrendered at Appomatox, three companies of the Eighth Iowa Cavalry caught the Tannehill works in full blast and destroyed them. Solidified iron still remains in two of the furnaces.

Abandoned and never rebuilt, the old ironworks reverted to wilderness until 1969 when the state legislature ordered the site preserved to interpret the early Alabama iron industry.

The reconstructed Tannehill Furnaces form the centerpiece of Tannehill Historic State Park just south of Bessemer.

14

Ironmaster & Benefactor

According to an associate, Thomas Tennessee Hillman was "born and bred in a furnace." His grandfather had forged the Birmingham area's first iron at a site near Tannehill in 1830. Hillman's father, also an ironmaster, visited Birmingham and described the area as "the spot most favored for ironmaking in the world."

When he was 7 years old, Hillman was thrown from his pony and suffered severe spinal injuries. After spending six years as an invalid, he attended school near Nashville and later went to work for his father's Empire Furnace Co. in Triggs County, Tennessee. During the Civil War, he was in charge of both the Center and Empire Furnaces.

Early in 1879, he formed a partnership with Henry DeBardeleben to build a blast furnace in Birmingham. He named Birmingham's first furnace "Alice" after his partner's daughter.

The output from Alice Furnace set new records for Alabama iron production from the start. Under Hill-man's expert guidance, the plant became a celebrated landmark in the city's development of an iron industry. Hillman later became a generous benefactor to the city's First Methodist Church and its first hospital.

T. T. Hillman (1844-1905)

Considered the oldest hospital in Birmingham, Hillman Hospital was established in 1902 and named in honor of its benefactor, T. T. Hillman. This photograph shows the hospital, at 20th Street and Sixth Avenue South, in 1929. It is now part of the University of Alabama at Birmingham (UAB) Medical Center.

Railroad Man & Iron Mogul

James Withers Sloss (1820-1890)

James Sloss was born on his father's farm in northern Alabama. At the age of 15, he went to work as a bookkeeper for a butcher in Florence.

After saving for seven years, he bought a small country store in Athens. With a good business sense and a charming Irish manner, he soon began to prosper. By the late 1850s, he had extended his mercantile business throughout northern Alabama. Sloss also owned several plantations and was active in railroad construction.

In 1871, the L. & N. Railroad accepted his proposition to complete the final gap of the track running between Decatur and Birmingham. Later, his business interests became centered in the Birmingham area, where he focused on the development of industrial operations.

His Sloss Furnace Co. was organized in 1881. One year later, the first furnace began producing "Sloss" brand pig iron. For the next 90 years, Sloss Furnaces produced much of the iron that fueled America's growth as an industrial nation. In 1977, Sloss Furnaces became a museum of the City of Birmingham. The furnaces are now silent, but blacksmiths and artists, working on the site, continue to fashion objects from iron. The 32-acre site is open to the public year round for tours, exhibits, community events, and special programs.

Birmingham's only National Historic Landmark, Sloss Furnaces is also the only 20th century industrial plant under preservation in the world. This photo shows the furnaces pouring iron around 1935. Today they showcase Birmingham ironmaking to visitors from around the world.

Ironworker & Town Builder

Samuel Thomas was born into a Welsh family of ironmakers. His father, David, had pioneered the manufacture of iron using anthracite coal as fuel. News of his discovery soon spread all over England and the United States. Pennsylvania businessmen convinced the elder Thomas to move there in 1839. This move hastened the rise of Pennsylvania's iron industry.

Young Samuel followed the career in which his family had been so successful. At the age of 16, he went to work in his father's blacksmith shop and learned the iron business from the ground up.

By 1865 he was serving as president of the Thomas Iron Co., the leading American iron manufacturer. Thomas also headed a group of Pennsylvania capitalists who began purchasing mineral lands in the area where Birmingham soon would be established. They formed the Pioneer Mining and Manufacturing Co. to oversee their holdings in Alabama.

Waiting until the city's iron industry was firmly established and booming, Samuel Thomas, and his son Edwin built two state of the art blast furnaces at Thomas, Alabama. They also planned and developed an industrial town nearby, with housing, church and commissary facilities identical to those of their Pennsylvania counterparts. At the turn of the century, Thomas's Alabama properties were merged into Republic Steel. The Thomas furnace community later became a neighborhood of the city of Birmingham.

Samuel Thomas and other family members

Laid out along tree-lined streets, the town of Thomas, with its Pennsylvania-style worker housing, is a National Register Historic District and the city's best-preserved industrial community.

Generous Providers

Newlyweds Vincent and Theresa Bruno left their native Sicily because it offered them a future no brighter than working another's land. Friends and relatives had come to America and written of work and opportunity here. In 1908, the young couple arrived in Birmingham. Vincent found employment at the Thomas furnaces and moved his bride into one of many company-built, three-room shotgun houses in the Thomas community.

By scrimping and saving, the Brunos bought an acre of land at the edge of the company town. Their "farm" not only fed their rapidly growing family, it fulfilled their dream of becoming landowners. In 1929, when Vincent was laid off, Theresa and the eight children pitched in. The oldest boys, Joe and Sam, went to work before and after school at nearby grocery stores. The entire family worked the land, caring for the garden, the cow and the chickens.

The Bruno kitchen was always open to homeless men who arrived daily on freight trains, begging a meal. Theresa fed them at her table, usually a zesty vegetable stew and fresh Italian bread. If one of the children asked who the stranger was, she would reply:

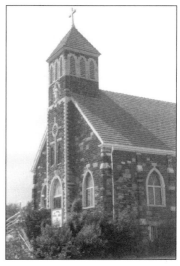

St. Mark's Catholic Church at Thomas, still a center of Birmingham's Italian community

"Chi sa. Non fa niente. Aveva appetito." ("Who knows. It doesn't matter. He was hungry.")

In 1932, during the height of the Depression, the Brunos invested their entire savings in a business venture. They opened a small store with this creed: "The customer is king." At a time when most grocery items were individually gathered, weighed and packaged, the Brunos did that and delivered the goods at no extra cost. The personal service, together with their quality products, turned their tiny 20-foot by 40-foot store into a profitable venture, one that has grown to be one of Alabama's largest and most successful corporations.

Vincent and Theresa Bruno

Hospitality Greek Style

Vasilios Demetrios ("Bill") Koikos (1894-1988)

At age 25 when many of his contemporaries in the small Greek village of Peleta were starting new lives as husbands and fathers, Vasilios (Bill) Koikos said goodbye to his sister, two brothers, and widowed mother.

Bill embarked on a journey that would take him —by foot, boat, train and streetcar— to a land where even the poorest citizens could still make their dreams come true.

Founded in 1907 by the Bonduris family, the Bright Star Restaurant, at 304 19th Street, Bessemer, still serves up good food with a warm welcome.

When he stepped off the streetcar in Bessemer, in the spring of 1920, Bill found the town and surrounding mining communities in full bloom. Coal and ore mines, pipe and railroad car plants were operating around the clock.

The day after his arrival, he took a job as a busboy at the Bright Star Restaurant. Every month he sent his entire paycheck of $40 home to his family. He lived off the tips given to him in appreciation of good service. Less than five years later, he had saved enough to become part owner in the restaurant. The Bright Star prospered as a Koikos family business and became internationally known for its excellent food and its hospitality.

An old Greek adage says that the culinary art is as important as any of the other arts, and a more consistent bringer of pleasure. To this day, the Koikos family keeps this culinary art alive at the Bright Star.

An Old World Community

St. Nicholas Russian Orthodox Church

During the 1880s, coal mining communities sprang up around Birmingham, many of them populated by European immigrants eager to start a new life in the land of freedom and opportunity. Those who came first would work hard and save enough to send money back to their homeland so that family, friends, and loved ones could buy passage to what seemed the promised land.

By 1910, the coal mining community of Brookside, Alabama had a population of 700, the majority of them Slovaks and eastern Europeans. To this small hillside village, they transplanted their customs and beliefs.

Brookside is thought to be among the first communities in the South settled by eastern European immigrants. The Russian Orthodox church at Brookside, still standing with its Byzantine-style copper dome, is one of Alabama's religious treasures. While the mines were open and the community was thriving, it was also a center of community activities.

Wedding celebrations were major events for members of all churches. The ethnic population was so large that the mines would close to accommodate the festivities.

Brookside's diverse ethnic groups got along well. According to one former resident, the groups harmonized "because (they) had to, (they) were all in the same boat."

Old World roots did not prevent the citizens of Brookside from taking pride in the mining town's modern conveniences. One man recalled the town's amenities: "We had everything: an ice plant, two movies, three or four doctors, two drugstores, and a blacksmith. We had a main street that was covered." By the end of World War II, most major mines had closed. Young people went to the cities, where there was work and additional opportunity. Nonetheless, Brookside has survived, and the Russian Orthodox church remains in the quiet, former mining center.

A First Communion class at St. Michael's in the early 20th century.

Engineer & Investor

Edward Magruder Tutwiler (1846-1925)

Edward Magruder Tutwiler was 18 years old when he left the Virginia Military Institute to volunteer for service in the Civil War. Many of his classmates were killed while attempting to stop the advance of the Union Army into Virginia. Tutwiler continued to serve on front lines until the end of the war.

After the war, Tutwiler returned to V.M.I. and graduated in 1867 with a degree in civil engineering. After teaching for two years, he became a rodman on a railroad crew in Pennsylvania.

His intelligence and capacity for hard work helped him rise rapidly. Soon he served as a locating, and later chief engineer for several rail lines in Ohio and Virginia. His association with the Georgia Pacific (later the Southern) Railway brought him to Birmingham in 1881.

Two years later, Tutwiler changed careers and became general superintendent of mining enterprises at Cardiff, Brookside, Blossburg and Brazil in the Warrior coal fields, which are located to the northwest of Birmingham. In 1889, he organized his own mining and manufacturing company, Tutwiler Coal, Coke & Iron Co.

In 1906, at age 60, Tutwiler retired from active business. He invested his industrial fortune in downtown real estate, including the grandiose Tutwiler Hotel (1913-1976) on 20th Street and the Ridgely Apartments on 21st Street at Park Place.

The historic Ridgely Apartments, recently renovated as a luxury-class hotel and restaurant, now serve as The Tutwiler, a major Birmingham business and social center.

Mining Prodigy

Erskine Ramsay (1864-1953)

According to his mother, Erskine Ramsay at age three sank a tiny shaft in the front yard, devised a cage, built a tipple and hoisted coal from his small mine. An original thinker, he was an inventor and loved to tinker with machinery.

Born in 1864 in Pennsylvania, he came from Scottish families that had worked in coal mines for more than 200 years. At age 12, Erskine followed suit, quickly working his way up from the maintenance shops to the company offices. In 1883, 19 year old Ramsay was made superintendent and engineer of mines and coke works owned by the H. C. Frick Coke Co. Three years later, his ability to increase coke production landed him the job of construction chief for one of the largest coke works in the world.

Ramsay moved to Alabama in 1887, when he became superintendent and engineer of the Tennessee Coal, Iron and Railroad Co.'s Pratt mines. The next year, Ramsay's division produced more than two million tons of coal, more than half the state output. At the astonishingly young age of 30, Ramsay was promoted to chief engineer of TCI. The new chief left his mark on America's coal mining industry. His inventive nature changed and improved the performance of mine ventilation, washing machinery, tracks, cars, tipples, screens and every other step in the mining process. He received patents for many of his inventions. Ramsay also speculated in real estate in Pratt City and Ensley, building the classically-styled Bank of Ensley, which remains at Ave. E and 19th St. in Ensley.

Ramsay's civic contributions to Birmingham were as impressive as his professional accomplishments. From 1922 to 1940, he was president of the Birmingham Board of Education. The city's schools flourished under his guidance as had the coal industry.

Ramsay High School on the city's Southside, completed in 1931, honors inventor, coal operator, philanthropist and school board president Erskine Ramsay.

King of the Southern Iron World

Henry Fairchild DeBardeleben was born on a farm near Montgomery in 1840. After his father died, 10 year old DeBardeleben went to work for a bakeshop. At age 16, he became the ward of Daniel Pratt, Alabama's leading industrialist at that time.

DeBardeleben moved to Prattville where he attended school and eventually managed the mill in which Pratt made cotton gins. Although opposed to secession, DeBardeleben joined the Confederate Army and served at the front line before being detailed to run the bobbin factory in Prattville for the Confederate government. In 1862, DeBardeleben married Ellen Pratt, Pratt's only child. During the next decade, his father-in-law relied more and more on DeBardeleben's business abilities.

In 1872, Pratt and DeBardeleben focused their attention on development of mineral resources in the Birmingham area. They bought a controlling interest in the Red Mountain

*Henry Fairchild DeBardeleben
(1840-1910)*

Coal and Iron Company, which successfully revived the Civil War iron works at Oxmoor. At Pratt's death in 1873, DeBardeleben became the one-big-moneyed man in Alabama. He poured this fortune, his tremendous energy and creative intelligence into all he did. He formed coal companies, started furnaces, founded the city of Bessemer, and in his own words, delighted in "getting things rolling." His properties became the nucleus of the U.S. Steel (now USX) Birmingham holdings.

DeBardeleben's keen business sense and charisma induced others to invest in the industrial development of Birmingham. By 1910, the year of his death, Birmingham had become the industrial capital of the South.

*DeBardeleben promoted the development of the Alice Furnace,
Birmingham's first iron furnace, which he named for his daughter.*

Iron Colossus

In 1903, two members of Birmingham's Chamber of Commerce, Fred Jackson and James MacKnight, came up with an idea to showcase Birmingham's industrial prowess in the national limelight.

They envisioned a colossal statue, cast from Alabama iron, that would become the city's exhibit at the World's Fair in St. Louis. With the fair only seven months away, Jackson and MacKnight worked hard to accomplish their task.

To symbolize their vigorous industrial city, they chose Vulcan, the multi-talented Roman god who was blacksmith, architect and armorer. Nationally prominent sculptor Giuseppe Moretti was commissioned to design the statue. Intrigued by the request, Moretti agreed to deliver the statue in time for the fair. James R. McWane undertook the casting.

At 55 feet, the giganitic iron man towered over all other exhibits at the fair, and although erected after opening day, won the grand prize.

In 1903, Birmingham foundrymen and promoters commissioned the great iron man to symbolize this city's industrial might.

For the next 30 years, Vulcan welcomed visitors to the Alabama Fairgrounds. In 1939, he was reassembled at his present site on Red Mountain where he has become the city's most prominent landmark. Vulcan's pedestal and observation platform offer visitors breathtaking views of the greater Birmingham area.

Vulcan at the Fairgrounds in the 1930s.

Entrepreneuse Extraordinaire

Peter and Rosa Zinszer moved to Birmingham from Kentucky in 1884. They opened their first store on 21st Street and sold "a few pictures and articles of furniture." Three years later, the Zinszers' business had outgrown its original location. They offered every possible home furnishing item to residents of the booming industrial city and were the first merchants to offer "easy payment," an early version of credit.

By 1889, their business occupied an immense cast-iron fronted store, still a landmark today at 2117 Second Ave. North. The success of their business was the result of hard work and an imaginative advertising campaign that included ads in both English and German language newspapers.

After Peter's death in 1895, it was Rosa who gave the store its memorable name, PETER ZINSZER'S MAMMOUTH FURNITURE HOUSE. Her newspaper ads were highly creative, as well. One read: "A pair of young lovers. The young man loves the young girl. The young girl loves the young man . . . and that is her thing. Together they will need many things. At Zinszer's, we have many of the things they will need."

After spending 32 years as one of Birmingham's most clever and successful businesswomen, Zinszer retired in 1915.

Rosa Zinszer (1858-1930)

Peter Zinszer constructed this elaborate "palace of trade" as the city's first and largest "easy payment" furniture house. Recently restored as offices for a law firm, the structure is Birmingham's finest example of a cast-iron front building. The entire facade is made of classically detailed cast iron and glass.

Burghard Steiner (1856-1923)

Financial Wizard

Burghard Steiner was born in the kingdom of Bohemia, now a province of Czechoslovakia. After finishing college in Pilsen, Steiner immigrated to Uniontown, Alabama, in 1875. The next year, his brother Sigfried finished his own education and joined his brother in Uniontown. The two then moved to Hamburg, Alabama, where Burghard's business skills soon became known to all.

In 1888, 33 year old Burghard and his brother moved to Birmingham and opened Steiner Brothers, a bank that specialized in investment transactions. The Steiner brothers rapidly established themselves as leaders in buying and selling real estate mortgages as well as state, city and county bonds. Steiner Brothers created an outside market for Birmingham real estate mortgages, convincing investors from all over America and Europe to help Birmingham grow.

Perhaps the largest contribution Steiner Brothers made to the young city was developing the plan that kept Birmingham from going bankrupt during the term of Mayor James Van Hoose in the 1890s. Because of an inadequate tax structure, the city found itself unable to pay full interest on the debt it owed its investors. During this crisis, the Steiner brothers convinced bondholders of the city, both in this country and in Europe, to accept a plan to give the city more time to pay the debt along with full interest. Some claim that the "Steiner Plan" introduced the concept of deferred interest to the investment banking world. Three successive generations of Steiner brothers managed Steiner banking in this city.

Built in 1890 at First Ave. N. and 21st St., the Steiner Building originally housed the banking chambers of Steiner Brothers as well as offices for architects and businessmen.

26

Pastor & Banker

W. R. Pettiford was born on his father's North Carolina farm in 1847. In his youth he worked for a tanner, then returned home to run the farm. In 1868, at the age of 21, Pettiford, who was then serving as a clerk in the Baptist church of Rocksboro, realized he had been called to spread the Gospel.

By 1877, Pettiford's theological studies had led him to Selma University, where he became a member of the school's pioneer faculty. As an instructor, Pettiford was remembered by students and co-workers alike as a well-spoken, patient man who taught the advantages of hard work by example. He was also one of the most successful fundraisers the University ever had.

After marrying Della Boyd of Selma, Pettiford left professorship for a pastor's duties at 16th Street Baptist Church in Birmingham. Soon the Baptist pastor saw that many black workers employed in the area needed financial as well as spiritual advice.

In 1890, the progressive clergyman organized the Alabama Penny Savings and Loan Association. With the help of other black leaders, Pettiford raised $25,000 in capital. He then travelled the back roads of the area, personally convincing rural blacks of the advantages of saving.

By 1907, Alabama Penny Savings had branches in Selma, Anniston and Montgomery and had helped more than 1,000 black families build their own homes. It had also become the second largest black-owned bank in America.

William R. Pettiford (1847-1914)

The Alabama Penny Savings Bank Building at 310 18th St. North, built in 1913, now serves as headquarters for the Knights of Pythias and houses a collection of business leader A. G. Gaston's memorabilia.

27

Banker & Builder

Christian Enslen immigrated to Montgomery from Germany in 1845. After fighting as a private in the Alabama Rifles during the Mexican War, he returned to Montgomery and learned blacksmithing skills. He later moved to Wetumpka and opened his own business. It was there that his son, Eugene, was born in 1858.

While Eugene was still a child, Christian joined the Confederate Army and served as a supervisor of blacksmiths, turning out thousands of horseshoes for the cavalry. After the war he tried his hand at railroading, then moved to Birmingham where he opened a retail business. Young Eugene went to work for his father as a clerk after attending Eastman College in Poughkeepsie, New York.

In less than seven years, the Enslens had saved enough money to open their own bank. A four-story brick building was erected on the corner of Second Avenue and 21st Street at a cost of $7,500.

In November of 1885, the business was incorporated under the name of C.F. Enslen and Sons, with Christian as president and Eugene as cashier.

Showing the typical German frugality that allowed him to prosper, Eugene Enslen personally supervised the laying of his bank's (the current City Federal Savings Bank Building's) foundation.

For the next 25 years, Eugene labored in his father's shadow and the bank prospered – so much so that he built an elegant Classical Revival style house for his family at 2737 Highland Avenue. This magnificent residence was known for decades on Southside as "the Marble Palace."

When his father retired in 1911, Eugene became president and immediately set out to leave his own mark on the business. He built a colossal and finely detailed 25-story office tower just across the street from the old bank, a building known for years as the Jefferson County Savings Bank.

28

Adventurous Architects

Charles Wheelock traveled extensively before he opened one of Birmingham's early architectural practices in 1883. He lived in Texas, New Mexico, California, and Emporia, Kansas, where he served as the city's first mayor.

Wheelock had his son Harry serve an apprenticeship as a carpenter before taking him in as a partner in 1888. At that time, many considered the Wheelocks the leading architectural firm in the city.

Their prolific practice included major public and commercial buildings, clubs, and residences. Some of their most successful designs were Craftsman and Colonial Revival style houses.

According to a family member, Harry Wheelock built his own Spanish Colonial Revival style house at 1500 19th Street South in response to a bet that he couldn't design and build a house on a lot that size.

Wheelock designs still standing include the original Hillman Hospital and Lakeview School, (both of 1901) and many residences in Birmingham's Rhodes Park and Southside districts.

The Wheelock father-and-son team designed this furniture and dry goods store at 2201 Second Avenue North which today bears their name. Its recent conversion to mixed-use condominiums serves both commercial and residential tenants.

Standing at a drafting table from left to right are Charles Wheelock, Harry Wheelock, and associates, including S. Scott Joy.

Contractor & "Sportin' Man"

Not much is known about T.C. Windham prior to his arrival in Birmingham in the 1910s; only that he came from Arkansas, where he had substantial business interests. It is known that he was already a man of considerable wealth who had great skills as a builder and contractor.

At the time of his arrival, many of the city's prominent black professional and white-collar workers lived in Smithfield, a community just to the west of the Birmingham city center. Windham soon bought a block of real estate in Smithfield and built a two-story brick mansion that reflected not only his wealth, but also his business abilities. Located on Eighth Avenue North, it featured the best contemporary craftsmanship, including elaborately carved woodwork, stained glass, and fine furnishings.

Working with his brother, R.L. Windham, Windham went on to build many other residences in the area. But it is the churches and commercial projects that now highlight the Windham construction legacy in Birmingham and throughout the South. The Masonic and Pythian

Windham Brothers Construction Co. built Sixteenth Street Baptist Church, designed by the black architect Wallace A. Rayfield.

Temples in the Fourth Avenue North National Register Historic District are outstanding examples of this work. In 1911, Windham built the Sixteenth Street Baptist Church on Sixteenth Street, the bombing of which would become one of the most tragic events in Birmingham's history.

According to a former neighbor, Windham was a "sportin' man," who delighted in all the material trappings of the very rich of his day. He had a uniformed chauffeur and a full complement of household servants. His daughters' weddings are remembered as events worthy of royalty.

T.C. Windham

Master Designer

William L. Welton was born on a Nebraska farm in 1874, just three years after Birmingham was founded. New citizens in what was then frontier territory, his parents were greenhorns to the wild west. Welton's father was a Boston merchant who, for some unknown reason, decided to live dangerously. But, by the time William was one year old, his family returned to Boston where his father resumed his original career.

Welton's architectural genius was recognized at Massachusetts Institute of Technology in Boston, where he studied architecture. After studying for two more years with leading professionals, Welton was awarded a travel scholarship to the Ecole des Beaux Arts in Paris. He also traveled to England, Switzerland, Italy, Greece, and Spain, studying the architectural heritage of those countries.

From 1902 to 1907, Welton worked for the major New York firm McKim, Meade and White, and was directly involved in the design of Pennsylvania Station and the Carnegie branch libraries in New York City.

In 1907, Welton came to Birmingham as a young associate working on the Empire Building at First Avenue North and 20th Street. After three years with a local partnership, he set out on his own. His firm handled many millions of dollars worth of work, including more than 500 residences, 10 apartment houses, eight churches, three theatres and numerous hotels, banks, stores, office buildings and warehouses. His largest single undertaking was the original Tutwiler Hotel on 20th Street. His personal residence is located at 3715 Cliff Road in Forest Park.

Welton supervised construction of the white terra-cotta clad Empire Building at First Ave. N. and 20th St., one of the early industrial city's most elaborate skyscrapers.

William Leslie Welton (1874-1934), and an associate

James Bowron, Jr. (1844-1928)

Industrialist & Chronicler

& Iron Company (TCI). But he also came with a writer's eye, and kept a chronicle of what he saw. This is how Bowron found Birmingham on his first visit:

"The O'Brien Opera House on the corner of First Ave. and 19th St. appeared to be outside the limit of the city. The Relay House had the ticket keeper's office and a room or two over it. A tin bowl and dipper was outside on the porch for anybody to wash. Where the Morris Hotel now stands was a big frog pond (lots of croaking)."

In 1899, Bowron wrote this simple paragraph about the progress he had witnessed in the United States: "Today I had my first experience of talking over long distance telephone. It is difficult for the present generation to realize that when I moved from England to this country, there was not a telephone or electric light or a dynamo or an electric power station of any sort in existence in the world."

"I found on coming to Birmingham that to be in the iron trade was to be respectable. To be an officer of an iron-making corporation was to have an entree to the best society, but to be the chief residential officer of the largest corporation was to carry the key to the kingdom of heaven." This passage from James Bowron's autobiography is typical of his writing style: highly descriptive and to the point.

Born in England in 1844, Bowron was instructed in the Quaker faith by his parents and teachers. Although he chose a career in the business world, he always took pleasure in writing. When he moved to Birmingham in 1883, he was secretary and treasurer of the Tennessee Coal

These skyscrapers at First Ave. and 20th St., then called the Heaviest Corner on Earth, housed Birmingham's early industrial corporations.

Real Estate Entrepreneur & Soldier

Louis Verdier Clark (1862-1934)

In 1906, Clark brought vaudeville to Birmingham with the construction of the Lyric Theatre and office building, still located at 18th Street and Third Avenue North.

A native of Marietta, Ga., Louis Clark grew up in Mobile and graduated from the University of Alabama in 1885. He spent the next year seeing the world as first mate on the "S.S. Ismar." In 1887, he settled in Birmingham and started a real estate and insurance firm.

Clark had been captain of cadets at the University. He continued his interest in military affairs by organizing the Jefferson Volunteer Company, which was later made part of the National Guard. The troops under his command were activated during the Hawes riots of 1888 and the miners' strikes of the 1890s.

In 1897, he was appointed brigadier general of the Alabama National Guard. He retired from that office in 1913, but when his former company was activated to serve in France during World War I, the 56 year old Clark offered his services. Rejected because of physical disabilities, he instead joined the Red Cross and was about to sail for France when the Armistice was signed.

Clark the businessman did much to help develop the city of Birmingham. He owned and operated many prime commercial buildings in the city center, including the Lyric Theater. When he built that structure in 1906, it showcased his innovative business ideas. Not only was it advanced in terms of reinforced concrete construction and technology, it also mixed two enterprises under one roof — a theater and commercial offices — which was a new concept at the time.

Clark's public spirit was as exceptional as his professional expertise. He took great interest in the civic and social welfare of the city. A quiet and unostentatious man, Clark's numerous and anonymous charitable contributions to Birmingham include the Clark Theatre on Birmingham's Southside.

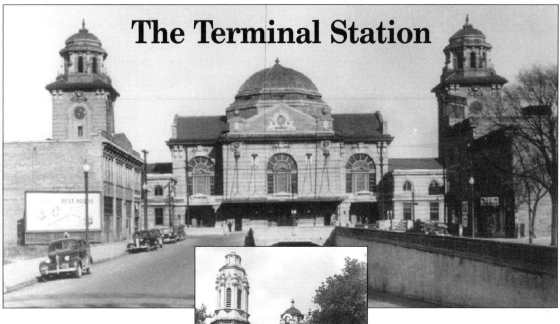

The Terminal Station

In the golden age of railroads, Birmingham's Terminal Station was the most elaborate passenger facility in the South. It was fitting that this great station was built in Birmingham, as the city's volume of rail traffic surpassed that of all other southern cities.

When it opened in 1909, men wearing spats and women in sweeping skirts walked beneath its ornamental glass dome. Marble walls, stairs, and dark oak benches completed the elegant interior furnishings.

The station was always busy. As soon as the departure of one train was announced, another pulled in. It was the industrial city's center of activity.

A newspaper headline of the day called it a "dream come true." It was beautiful and efficient, too.

But as the importance of rail travel began to fade, so did the prominence of the Terminal Station. The once beautiful building became run-down and was viewed by many as a dirty

The Terminal Station (1909-1969)

P. Thornton Marie, architect for the Terminal Station, also designed Highlands Methodist Church. The Five Points landmark's dome, towers and buff brick exterior are reminiscent of the city's most cherished landmark.

monstrosity. In 1969, 60 years after it opened, energetic developers demolished the station to prepare the site for construction of a federal building that rose on another site in the city center. The station site, just east of 26th Street at Fifth Avenue North, remains vacant today.

True Tales

OF BIRMINGHAM

Journalist & Historian

When Ethel Armes arrived in the early 1900s, Birmingham was one of the most rapidly developing and progressive cities in the nation.

The daughter of an Army officer, Armes had spent many years in isolated Western outposts where she learned the rough-and-tumble life-style of mining and industrial communities. An accomplished journalist, she had worked as a reporter and features writer for *The Washington Post* and *The Chicago Chronicle* before joining the staff of *The Birmingham Age-Herald.* After her Birmingham career, she wrote for *The Boston Herald* and published a history of the Lee family of Virginia and Stratford Hall. In 1907, the Birmingham Chamber of Commerce commissioned Armes to write a history of Alabama's coal and iron industries. A diligent and meticulous researcher, she put on a miner's cap

and inspected coal and iron ore sites and communities across the northern Alabama mineral region. She gathered photographs and records and conducted hundreds of interviews with industrial leaders.

Armes' book, *The Story of Coal and Iron in Alabama,* published in 1910, captures not only the facts surrounding this remarkable era in the region's growth, but also the personalities who made it happen.

Ethel Armes (b. 1876)

In 1910, the Birmingham Chamber of Commerce, with its "Trade in Birmingham" sign atop its office tower at First Avenue North and 19th Street, promoted the industrial city through Armes' history.

Enlightened Industrialist

John Joseph Eagan (1870 - 1924)

John Joseph Eagan was the principal founder and first president of the American Cast Iron Pipe Company (ACIPCO), established in 1905. Eagan was a successful businessman and industrialist and was also a Christian layman who firmly believed in translating religious beliefs into corporate policy.

In 1910, acting on his desire to instill in his associates the ideal of sharing, Eagan offered key employees of the pipe plant 10 shares of company stock as a reward for remaining with the organization for five years.

One year later, he formally inaugurated an enlightened program of employee benefits. This program included medical services, banking and pension plans, and bonuses awarded to employees who worked every day in the year. In 1913, ACIPCO built a three-story "civic center" for employees and their families. The center also served the surrounding community.

Shortly before his death in 1924, Eagan created a plan for employees to become involved in management of company affairs. He also designed a profit-sharing program.

John Joseph Eagan's faith in employee cooperation resulted in plans and programs that were decades ahead of their time.

In the early decades of this century, Birmingham became the center of America's cast iron pipe industry, with ACIPCO's North Birmingham Plant, then and now, one of the nation and the world's largest producers.

Educator & Social Worker

Sue Bertha Coleman's mother was working as a cook for a Huntsville family when she decided her daughter should have a college education, something few Alabama women achieved at the turn of the century.

Coleman graduated from Fisk University in Nashville. She began her career as principal of a Tennessee Coal and Iron Company (TCI) school at Muscoda, a large ore mining camp near Bessemer. At the end of her third year, she remained on the company's summer payroll to conduct social work for the families at this mining community.

Although she had no formal training in social work, Coleman was designated as a community supervisor in charge of social services for black miners and their families. Initiative and dedication set her apart from her

*Sue Bertha Coleman
(1875 - 1949)*

peers. In 1918, she borrowed $300 from a bank, left her husband in charge of their children, and went to Chicago to study with Jane Addams, the most noted social worker of the day.

On her return, Coleman took over a schedule of regular weekly duties at the "Colored Community House" that kept her busy from dawn to dusk. Whether it was teaching children to read and write, or their mothers to cook and sew, Sue Bertha Coleman helped the people in the ore mining camp of Muscoda learn the responsibilities of neighbors and community.

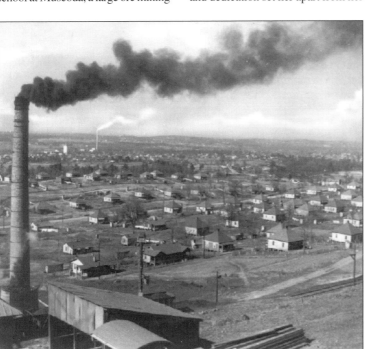

Many of the TCI ore miners' houses, pictured in this 1937 photograph, remain today along the Wenonah - Ishkooda Road near Bessemer.

Social Worker & Executive

Winifred Collins, born in Knoxville, Illinois, studied home economics and social work in Chicago and received several graduate degrees by 1911. Collins volunteered her services as a teacher of the immigrants at the famous settlement houses in this city in exchange for room and board, and became director of home economics by the time she received her social work degrees.

In 1917, she turned down a job in Washington, D.C. and came to Birmingham to take the position of superintendent of the Tennessee Coal and Iron Company's Social Science Department. Collins worked as the only woman filling an administrative position in the male-dominated TCI corporate structure. In this capacity she developed one of the most extensive corporate welfare systems

Winifred Collins (d. 1941)

in the country. At its peak in the mid-1920s, her department employed 300 people who worked with over 30,000 people in TCI's 23 schools, industrial camps and community centers. Her field workers taught home economics, education, gardening, recreation and other subjects to employees and their families.

TCI built substantial residences for teachers at its many camps, including this cottage at Johns, thought to be one of the last remaining.

Pioneer Educator

John Herbert Phillips (1853-1921)

One rainy night in 1883, Mayor A. O. Lane and seven of Birmingham's eight Aldermen met in a room charged with emotion. Lane and three of the Aldermen present wanted the 30 year old Ohio native, John Herbert Phillips, to take charge of the city's school system. The other four Alderman were against Phillips. They feared he would "yankeeize" the schools and make education available to all Birmingham's children, a controversial issue in the late 19th century South.

At this time Birmingham's 2,000 residents had neither paved streets nor street lights, so when the missing Alderman finally arrived, he held a lantern in his hand. Lane quickly called the vote and broke the four-to-four tie. Thus, Birmingham elected Phillips Superintendent of Schools.

For the next 38 years, Phillips worked tirelessly to develop and expand every branch of the city's educational institutions. Not content to provide schools for the city's young of all races and religions, Phillips also founded the Birmingham Public Library and the Booker T. Washington branch for blacks.

Largely because of Phillips' ability to overcome obstacles and financial handicaps, *The Journal of Education*, a national publication, praised the Birmingham school system, saying it "had attained a place of distinction in the educational world." The editor of the journal credited Phillips' educational vision, which considered the individual child and his needs as the hub of the wheel of which teachers, curriculum and facilities form the spokes. But for the arrival of a single Alderman, lantern in hand, one of Birmingham's most enlightening citizens might have been lost to the city and our history set on a darker course.

Phillips High School, constructed in 1923 and named for Phillips, Superintendent of Schools, 1883-1921.

Educators & Humanitarians

Born in Eufaula, Alabama, Carrie Tuggle was the daughter of a Mohawk chief and a former slave. Around the turn of the century, she moved to Birmingham in search of a career.

She became a social worker and counseled delinquent boys, often appearing with them in court. At that time juveniles were tried in the same court as adults. Mrs. Tuggle saw the injustice of this situation and was instrumental in the formation of the Jefferson County Juvenile and Domestic Court.

In 1903, she formed the Tuggle Institute in Enon Ridge as a school and residence for homeless boys. From a modest start, the Institute became an important factor in the advancement of Blacks. Outstanding graduates from Tuggle include businessman Dr. A. G. Gaston, and musicians John T. ("Fess") Whatley and Erskine Hawkins.

The Birmingham Board of Education purchased Tuggle Institute in 1934 and later named it Tuggle Elementary School. Other city of Birmingham schools named for prominent black educators include the Scott School in Pratt City, Hayes School in Avondale and Parker (originally Industrial High) School in Smithfield.

Carrie A. Tuggle (1858-1924)

Carol William Hayes (1897-1988)

George W. Scott (1873-1934)

Arthur H. Parker (1870-1939)

Public Servant & Poet

Samuel Ullman was born in Europe in 1841. At age 11, he immigrated to Port Gibson, Mississippi. At the outbreak of the Civil War, he enlisted in the Army of Virginia and was severely wounded at the battle of Cold Harbor.

By the time he moved to Birmingham in 1884, the 43 year old Ullman owned his own hardware business, and soon became known as an outstanding leader in religious and educational circles. Soon after arriving here, he became a member of Birmingham's first board of education and was its president from 1893 to 1900. So respected was Ullman for his spiritual guidance that he became a "lay" rabbi at the request of the Temple Emanu-El congregation in 1890. After three decades of public service, Ullman retired and turned his active mind to poetry. In 1918, at age 77, he wrote a poem entitled *Youth*. Even though this poem was published on a small scale, it has had a profound effect on many readers around the world, including General Douglas

Education at the University of Alabama at Birmingham continues in Ullman Elementary School's classrooms and offices.

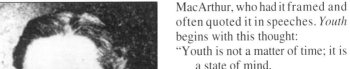

MacArthur, who had it framed and often quoted it in speeches. *Youth* begins with this thought:

"Youth is not a matter of time; it is a state of mind,
  it is not a matter of rosy cheeks, red lips and supple knees;
  it is a matter of the will, a quality of the imagination, a vigor of the emotions;
  it is the freshness of the deep springs of life."

Samuel Ullman (1841-1924)

Richard Massey (1867-1949)

Educator & Businessman

Stylishly bedecked with polychrome-terra-cotta flourishes, the 10-story Massey Building typifies the optimism of its builder and business conditions in the 1920s.

Richard W. Massey arrived in Birmingham in 1887 with little more than his lunch and a letter of introduction. A short time later he rented a typewriter and a room, and with the enrollment of six male students started the Massey Business College, "to train intellects for commercial service." He wanted to teach business to southern farmers.

From this simple beginning, Massey developed a network of business colleges throughout the southeast. His Birmingham College, recently renovated at 2024 Third Ave. North, served as the architectural model for these colleges.

Massey's energy and resourcefulness soon extended far beyond his business schools. He successfully dabbled in real estate investment and by 1905 moved his family into one of the city's most magnificent homes. His Highland Avenue estate featured formal Italian gardens, with statuary and fountains, which European gardeners tended with great care.

In the 1920s, Massey built a highly ornamental Spanish-style office building across the street from his business college. Always keeping up with (or ahead of) the times, he was one of the first to move to the newly emerging community of Mountain Brook Estates. His Spanish-style mansion still remains along the Mountain Brook Parkway.

Scholar & Educator

M.P. Burley attended grammar and high school in his hometown of Macon, Ga..His love of learning guided him to Ballard Normal School, where he excelled in a broad range of subjects, including Latin. Even though he was an outstanding scholar, Burley could find no work in his chosen field as an educator, so he took a job at a soap factory until a better opportunity came along.

In the fall of 1903, he received a teaching job, but soon concluded that his own education was still incomplete. Burley then entered Atlanta University, where he finished college while supporting himself as a photographer during the summers.

After graduation in 1909, he was appointed Professor of English, Science, and Latin at Homer College. Six years later, he left his native state to become Professor of Science at Miles College in Birmingham. Burley's special talent for teaching was recognized by his promotion to President of Miles in 1927.

Never satisfied with his own knowledge of the latest educational advancements, Burley took

M.P. Burley

special post-graduate courses at the University of Pennsylvania every summer. Under Burley's leadership, Miles gained recognition as one of America's leading black colleges.

Established in 1908 in Fairfield, Miles College's physical facilities include Brown Hall, built under Burley's leadership.

City Librarian

When Lila May Chapman arrived in Birmingham in 1909, she had a six-month contract to help classify and catalog books in the city library. She ended up remaining with the library until her retirement as director in 1947.

Born in Dadeville, Alabama, Chapman was raised in Georgia and graduated from Wesleyan College there in 1890. When the Carnegie Library School opened, she was one of the first 10 students to enroll and was in the first graduating class.

While still a student, Chapman was sent to organize and catalog the books in the new Carnegie Library in Ensley. After graduating, she cataloged the books of the public library in Gadsden. She then worked two years as a librarian in Corsicana, Texas, before coming to Birmingham.

She later recalled that during her first summer in the Magic City, only 3,329 books were circulated, so she had plenty of time to classify books and prepare a card catalog. From that modest start she devoted the next 38 years to building a truly exceptional collection of books for the city.

During Lila May Chapman's career, the Birmingham Public Library grew to be the largest in Alabama and to be recognized as one of the great library systems in the nation.

Lila May Chapman (1872-1953)

The original Birmingham Public (now Linn-Henley Research) Library opened in April of 1927. Magnificently restored in 1986, its grandly classical entrance on Linn Park welcomes researchers and patrons. At the right, beneath the great glass gable is entrance to the city's Main Library constructed in the 1980s.

Maker of Musicians

John T. ("Fess") Whatley was a young child living in Tuscaloosa when he heard a passing circus street band. From that day on, he wanted to play the cornet. As a teenager, he entered Birmingham's Tuggle Institute and joined the band.

Long before Tuggle days, Whatley had been exploring a new style of music called jazz and developing his own soft sound that became known as the "Fess Whatley" tone.

In 1917, at age 20, Whatley became an instructor at Industrial (now Parker) High School in the Smithfield neighborhood. Here he organized the city's first black brass band. At this time, his students nicknamed him "Fess," short for "professor."

Whatley was a strict disciplinarian. With exceptional skill, he inspired and trained his students. During the 1930s and 1940s, big band leaders in northern cities such as Lionel Hampton and Duke Ellington telephoned Whatley when they needed a musician. They knew that a Whatley student could play like a professional.

"Fess" Whatley's Saxo-Society Band was one of many that played at dance halls and clubs like the one formerly located at Tuxedo Junction in the Ensley neighborhood.

Whatley's most famous student is Erskine Hawkins. This Birmingham musician-composer's hit tune "Tuxedo Junction," written in 1939, put the city on the map for jazz fans around the world.

Another Whatley pupil, J. L. Lowe, kept Birmingham's jazz heritage alive both as a musician and as principal founder of the Jazz Hall of Fame, located in the former Carver Theatre and the Fourth Avenue National Register Historic District.

*John T. ("Fess") Whatley
(1897-1971)*

Artist & Teacher

Hannah Elliott was Alabama's foremost painter of miniature portraits as well as a distinct individualist. Although trained in New York, Paris, and Rome, "Miss Hannah" was unconcerned with the styles and customs of the day. She dressed as she pleased. In her later days, she appeared only in a black dress, neck ribbon, black hat and tennis shoes. Although she was from a distinguished family, this independent southern lady lived simply through the help of generous patrons throughout her life.

Her studio was in a one-story house which was atop a steep hill near Five Points South. Inside, collections of rare books and family furnishings abounded. Busts, plaster casts, paintings and easels were everywhere. Her home was also a gathering place for several generations of painters and students of art appreciation.

"Miss Hannah" was one of the founders of the Birmingham Art Association, and her untiring efforts helped establish the city's art museum. She also taught in local private schools. Her student, Arthur Stewart, captured

Miss Hannah Elliott (1876-1951)

her in the watercolor portrait pictured above.

Prominent Birmingham lawyer Henry Upson Sims is said to have built the Florentine Building, at 21st Street and Second Avenue North, for "Miss Hannah". Its decorative terra-cotta ornament recalls Venetian palaces, which Sims and other students visited on "Miss Hannah's" European tours.

Brother to a City

James Alexander Bryan was born in South Carolina in 1863 while his father was serving with the Confederate Army in Virginia. As a youth, he received strict Presbyterian training. In 1880, he entered the University of North Carolina on a scholarship, and six years later attended Princeton Theological Seminary in New Jersey —again on a scholarship.

In 1888, Bryan spent his summer months at a small church on Birmingham's Southside conducting worship for industrial workers and their families. After graduating, he turned down an offer to serve a large church in Philadelphia and chose to pastor Birmingham's Third Presbyterian Church.

For the next 40 years, Bryan was the pastor of one of the smallest churches in the city, but his parish was by far the largest. He was constantly out on the streets and in the mills, factories and pool halls, ministering to an immigrant community which spoke 27 languages. During the five decades he served Birmingham's poor and needy, Bryan conquered prejudice with prayer and won the admiration of all. His piety and friendliness earned him the nickname "Brother" Bryan. When *The Birmingham News* awarded Bryan a "loving cup," Rabbi Morris Newfield of Temple Emanu-El said of him,

"He is the noblest, sweetest spirit I have ever known."

Before Bryan died in 1941, the people he served gave him one of the few things he desired for himself —a trip to the Holy Land.

Birmingham's beloved pastor ministered to the entire city from The Third Presbyterian Church at 617 22nd St. South.

The Rev. James Alexander ("Brother") Bryan in his well-known "calling" carriage, c. 1917.

Religious Leader

Reverend William M. Winters (d. 1943)

At the turn of the century, William M. Winters was a familiar sight in Southside's black community. He regularly drove his horse and buggy through the neighborhood making calls on the sick and needy.

In addition to earning the community's admiration, Winters also won the respect of local bankers and secured a construction loan for the Bethel Baptist Church. Members of the congregation had tried for more than three decades to build a permanent house of worship.

A tornado had destroyed their first church, built in 1886. Parishioners replaced it with a school house, which was transported via logs from a site near Magnolia Park. The effort interrupted streetcar service for a week.

But Winters still wanted to build a solid and substantial church in which his congregation could worship and take pride. As a result of many fish fry and barbecue fundraisers, as well as the loan he secured, his determination was finally rewarded.

In December 1930, the first service was held in the auditorium of the new brick Bethel Baptist Church building. Joining Reverend Winters on the celebration platform was his colleague from the Third Presbyterian Church just a few blocks away, the Reverend James ("Brother") Bryan.

Bethel Baptist Church, 824 23rd Street South in the Southside neighborhood.

Health Care Provider

Lloyd Noland (1880-1948)

When Dr. Lloyd Noland came to Birmingham in 1913, he was the chief surgeon for the Tennessee Coal and Iron Co. (TCI), U.S. Steel's southern subsidiary. Trained in Baltimore, Noland had served in the Panama Canal with several medical detachments from 1904 to 1913. In Birmingham, he soon became the first superintendent of TCI's growing department of health. At this time, the occurrence of malaria, typhoid, dysentery and smallpox was widespread. In fact, these diseases were effecting an unusually high employee turnover—almost 400 percent per year.

Under Noland's leadership, swamps and marshes throughout the company's mining and industrial camps were drained; sanitary waste disposal measures adopted, and food and milk inspections and other health measures put into practice. In his first active year, malaria cases dropped from 4,800 to 370. Four years later, there were only 30 cases evident.

In 1919, Noland convinced TCI to build a $1.3 million hospital, overlooking its Fairfield plants. Contemporaries described the industrial hospital, one of the first of its kind in the nation, as "the most magnificent of any of the institutions in the Birmingham District." The TCI hospital became a state leader in the provision of health care services.

Originally known as the TCI Employees' Hospital, this Fairfield landmark, still standing on its commanding Flint Ridge site, was re-named in 1950 to honor its founder and long-time medical director, Lloyd Noland.

Surgeon & Soldier

Arthur M. Brown was born in Raleigh, North Carolina in 1867. His grandmother was one of that city's early public schoolteachers, and his parents made sure that he received a good education.

*Arthur McKimmon Brown
(1867-1939)*

Brown's residence at 319 Fourth Terrace in the Smithfield neighborhood, currently serves as a community center.

In 1884, Brown was awarded a scholarship to Lincoln University in Lincoln, Illinois, where he excelled as a student and a singer, winning the Silver Leaf Glee Club Award. In 1891, he received an M.D. from the University of Michigan.

At age 24, Brown first opened his medical practice in Bessemer, later moving to Cleveland and Chicago before establishing himself as a surgeon in Birmingham in 1894. Dr. Brown was involved in a variety of civic activities, including service as chairman of the Alabama Prison Improvement Board. His wife, Nellie, also served her community as a caseworker for the Children's Aid Society.

When the Spanish-American War broke out in 1898, Brown organized a company of infantrymen and offered the group's services to the Alabama Governor. Although his group was not activated, Brown was commissioned a first lieutenant and served as a surgeon in Santiago, Cuba throughout the war.

Upon his return to Birmingham, his medical practice flourished. In 1906, black architect Wallace Rayfield designed a gracious residence in Smithfield for Dr. Brown and his family.

Political Activist

In 1910, Pattie Ruffner Jacobs attended a conference in Birmingham at which the Chicago social reformer, Jane Addams, spoke.

Always a strong-willed and independent woman, Jacobs devoted the next decade to leading the Alabama movement for women's suffrage.

Her compassion for humanity extended beyond voting rights for women. Several years after women's suffrage had been won, she spoke out against restrictions that prevented blacks from voting.

She also used her political influence to attack other injustices, such as leasing convicts and children to work in area coal mines and other industries.

Jacobs eventually became Alabama's first Democratic National Committeewoman and was appointed to head the woman's division of the Consumer Advisory Board of the National Recovery Administration, an important New Deal agency.

At the time of her death in 1935, Pattie Ruffner Jacobs managed the Tennessee Valley Authority's Birmingham office.

Pattie Ruffner Jacobs (1875-1935)

This 1912 photograph shows the 2800 block of Highland Avenue, home to many prominent Birmingham residents, including the indefatigable southern reformer, Pattie Ruffner Jacobs.

Mistress of the Mansion

Their romance was not the kind that gossips were likely to overlook. The bride was the eldest daughter of B.B. Comer, Alabama's "Great Education Governor." The groom was related to Jane Lathrop, wife of Capt. Miles Standish, the experienced leader of the Mayflower pilgrims. When they married in 1902, Sallie Comer was in her late twenties and Frank Lathrop was in his early fifties. Both had children by previous marriages.

When Sallie and Frank built a cottage at the rear of their property on 14th Avenue South and moved in with all their children, skeptics must have had a field day wondering how long such a relationship could last. But the large, if unconventional, Lathrop family lived together in those small quarters until their permanent residence was completed.

The size and beauty of the new mansion made it one of the city's premiere homes. In fact, during the early 1900s, many weddings took place at 1923 14th Avenue South because it was the perfect setting for elaborate functions. Lathrop, a lumber baron, spared no expense when it came to materials and skilled craftsmen. From its massive red oak staircase to the leaded glass doors of the kitchen cabinets, Sallie and Frank's home was a builder's masterpiece.

There they raised their own daughter, Eva Comer Lathrop, and lived happily until Frank's death in 1936, at the age of 85.

Sallie Comer Lathrop

---

*The Classical Revival style
Lathrop House, with its elaborate
embellishments outside and in.*

Arlington
Historic House & Museum

Sometime in the 1850s, William Mudd built Arlington. According to family tradition, the young attorney presented the Greek Revival style house to his bride as a wedding gift.

During the Civil War, Union troops invaded Jefferson County and, as Arlington served as headquarters for Gen. James H. Wilson, it escaped damage. Although the house survived, Reconstruction led to hard times and the house was sold in 1884.

The property changed hands several times before Robert S. Munger

William S. Mudd (1816-1884)

This photograph shows Robert Munger, right, and other Munger family members enjoying Arlington about 1910. Today, the historic house and grounds are open to the public year-round.

purchased it as a summer retreat in 1902. Munger, a Texas-born inventor and manufacturer of cotton gins, renamed it Arlington. He also began to subdivide the property surrounding the home. As his eight children married, he gave them homesites in the neighborhood.

In 1953, the City of Birmingham purchased the property to preserve one of its last remaining antebellum houses. Today, with its extensive furnishings and grounds, the restored Arlington offers visitors a glimpse of the fashionable life at the turn of the century.

Executive & Sports Fan

Born in 1876, the year the National Baseball League was founded, A.H. ("Rick") Woodward grew up to become one of the sport's biggest fans. As son of one of Birmingham's most prominent industrial families, Rick was destined to work his way up the corporate ladder at the Woodward Iron Co., but he never let business stand in the way of his boyhood dreams: playing baseball and becoming a railroad engineer.

While attending the University of the South and the Massachusetts Institute of Technology, Woodward also earned an engineer's license and played catcher on the school teams. His parents discouraged his interest in baseball, but even when Woodward started work as a leather wrapper at the family ironworks, he maintained an active interest in baseball and railroading.

In 1910, "Mr. Rick" built Birmingham's first baseball stadium, Rickwood Field, and gave professional baseball in the city a big lift. Many who knew him remember a

Today, Rick Woodward's Red Mountain residence is home to the President of the University of Alabama at Birmingham.

colorful, unforgettable character and a consummate sports fan, especially when it came to his team, the Birmingham Barons.

He was elected vice president of the Southern Association of Baseball Clubs, and in 1918, became chief executive of Woodward Iron. Through the years, he kept his engineer's license up to date, and it was not uncommon for the chairman of the board of Woodward Iron to take a run on the Atlanta, Birmingham and Atlantic Railroad.

Allen Harvey ("Rick") Woodward (1876-1950), fifth from left, back row, with the 1916 Birmingham Barons team.

The Fighting Mayor

George Ward grew up with Birmingham. In 1871, the year of the city's founding, he moved here with his parents. They were the owners of the Relay House, an early hotel located near the railway passenger depot. At age 16, he left public school and became a runner for the First National Bank. Eventually he attended Cumberland University in Lebanon, Tenn., and returned to First National as a cashier in 1901. A year later he set out on his own as an investment banker and broker.

Ward entered city politics in 1899, a year before his 30th birthday. He served as an Alderman of the second ward for six years. In 1905, he was elected Mayor of Birmingham. He brought businesslike organization to City Hall. Known as the "Fighting Mayor" because of his war against saloons, crime and old-time political machines, Ward advanced the causes of education, police and fire protection, and urban planning. He was reelected in 1907, and in 1913 became the first elected President of the Birmingham Commission, the newly adopted form of city government.

During his first term as Commission President, Ward started the "City Beautiful" movement. He encouraged general fix-up/cleanup projects and landscaping. Women organized into block improvement societies.

Ward's country home on Shades Mountain replicated the Roman Temple of Vesta. A garden pavilion, the Temple of Sybil, remains at the U.S. 31 gateway to Vestavia Hills, a community named for the famous estate.

Gardening courses were taught at city schools where prizes were offered to school children for their beautification efforts. And planning was in the works to develop a civic and municipal complex at today's Linn Park. By 1916, more than 25,000 gardens bloomed in Birmingham. That year the *World Almanac* changed the city's epithet from "Magic City" to "City Beautiful."

When he retired from public office in 1918, a local newspaper offered Ward this tribute: "In courage, he is a skyscraper. His absolute independence has long been established. He typifies no particular interest, class or faction. He is a sincere, genuine and honest representative of all people."

George B. Ward (1870-1940)

Journalist & Civic Booster

Rufus N. Rhodes was born in Pascagoula, Miss. in 1856. His father was a prominent lawyer who had worked in the nation's capital, and young Rufus decided to follow in his footsteps. After attending public schools, he studied law, and was admitted to the bar at age 19. For the next 12 years, Rhodes enjoyed a

Rufus N. Rhodes (1856-1910)

successful career in law in Clarksville, Tennessee and Chicago before moving to Birmingham in 1887, at age 31. Here he became editor of the *Daily Herald.* When his boss objected to his first editorial campaign, Rhodes resigned and three days later launched his own newspaper, *The News.*

He set the tone for his paper with the slogan, "Great is Birmingham and *The News* is its prophet." This was a proud boast for a newspaper with four employees and a circulation of 628. No one could doubt that Rhodes believed in the greatness of Birmingham, and his enthusiasm served as a tonic its citizens needed on a daily basis. Two years later, circulation was up to 7,000, and by 1891, *The News* was the most widely read newspaper in the state.

As the paper grew, it changed names several times before becoming *The Birmingham News* in 1895.

In 1909 Rhodes sold the paper to Victor Hanson, a young man from Montgomery with a long history of journalistic experience. Four generations of the Hanson family have served as general managers and publishers of *The Birmingham News.*

The Birmingham News, *established in 1888, built this Jacobethian Revival style headquarters in 1916.*

Streetcar King

Robert Jemison Sr. (1853-1926)

Robert Jemison Sr. was born in Tuscaloosa in 1853. A graduate of the University of Alabama's first law class in 1874, Jemison spent 10 years in the hardware business.

In 1884, he moved to Birmingham where he established and became president of the East Lake Land Co. and Birmingham Union Street Railway. Jemison proved himself a masterful executive by consolidating nine competing streetcar lines, three electric light companies and one gas company into the Birmingham Railway, Light and Power Co. By 1900, this company managed 100 miles of streetcar track and five parks serving 10 million passengers annually. It was America's second largest streetcar railway system. The railway's power plant (at 19th St. and First Avenue South) and office building (at 21st and First Avenue North) remain today and provide steam heat and office space for city center businesses.

In 1898, Jemison formed City Land Co. and bought 40 acres on Red Mountain's northern slope. In 1899, he brought the nation's leading landscape architect, Samuel Brown Parsons of New York, to Birmingham to design a homeplace for himself and "a few congenial friends." He named it Glen Iris Park.

When Jemison died in 1926, a *Birmingham News* editorial, commenting on Jemison's wide-ranging business affairs and community leadership, concluded he was "not a chip off the old block but the old block itself."

Today Jemison's Greek Revival style house dominates the wooded Glen Iris National Register Historic District on the city's Southside.

Planner & Developer

Born in Tuscaloosa in 1878, Robert Jemison Jr. moved to Birmingham when he was six years old. He attended local public schools and spent two years at the University of Alabama and another two studying law at the University of the South in Sewanee, Tennessee.

In 1899, Jemison returned to Birmingham and entered the family hardware business. After four years, he decided to pursue a career that would have a profound effect on the growing industrial city – real estate.

In 1903, he organized the Jemison Real Estate and Insurance Co., quickly developing a fine reputation in this fast-growing field of business. Six years later, U.S. Steel asked Jemison to develop an entire town for the employees of its proposed new mills. Jemison hired a respected national land planner and traveled all over America and Europe studying

Robert Jemison Jr. (1878-1974)

models for industrial city planning. The resulting town of Fairfield, then called "Corey," set new standards for Birmingham development. President Theodore Roosevelt visited and praised the town's design at its dedication in March 1911.

Jemison's vision and dedication are responsible for most of the noteworthy land planning and residential development in Birmingham. The Jemison legacy also includes many office buildings in the city center and the subdivisions of Central Park, Forest Park, Redmont, Mountain Brook and Trussville.

Jemison's office is still preserved intact in this Renaissance Revival style building at 2115 Third Ave. North in the city center.

From Shepherd to Tycoon

Adolph B. Loveman (1844-1916)

Born in Hungary in 1844, Adolph Bernard Loveman spent the first two decades of his life as a farmer and shepherd. At age 21, he came to America and travelled as a peddler through Tennessee and Alabama. In 1870, he married Minnie Weil, a descendent of Spaniards who fled to America from the infamous Inquisition.

In 1877, 33 year old A.B. Loveman moved his family to Birmingham, where he opened a small dry goods business. His energetic manner and skill at supplying those items people most wanted to buy soon won the confidence of the public and Loveman's store expanded.

A decade later, in 1888, Loveman took into partnership M.V. Joseph of Selma. One year later, business continued to grow at a rate that warranted another expansion of management and Emil Leo Loeb joined the firm as partner. In 1890, the firm of Loveman, Joseph and Loeb bought for its future home what had once been the city's streetcar barn on the southwest corner of 19th Street near Third Avenue. The wisdom of choosing this central location is evidenced by a newspaper article written four decades later in 1930. It describes the store's site as "the hub of the business district and ... the very center of town."

Loveman's slogan, "Merchandise that Merits Confidence," was apparently more than a promise. For several generations, Loveman's remained Birmingham's largest and best-known department store.

The Loveman's Department Store building is still located at Third Avenue North and 19th Street. In its prime, Loveman's was an "immense shopping palace" that offered every possible household good, clothing and service under one roof. Loveman's is currently under renovation to house Discovery 2000, a hands-on science museum.

Mom Pop Management

Nazha Boohaker was a teenager in 1913 when she and her husband, Abdalla, came to Birmingham from Lebanon. They lived with other Lebanese immigrants on Birmingham's Southside in tiny houses, where only the bedrooms weren't shared. Abdalla became a peddler, carrying a pack and showing his dry goods to customers whose language he did not yet understand.

After seven years of hard work and saving, Abdalla opened his own grocery store on 13th Street South. As Abdalla and his growing family prospered in their successful Birmingham store, other Lebanese immigrants remarked of them that "the earth they touched turned to gold."

In 1923, the Boohaker family returned to Lebanon and bought a farm, but after living in America, farm life seemed slow and unchallenging. Two years later, the family returned to Birmingham.

Abdalla then bought a grocery store which he, his wife, and the older children operated. In 1937, while revisiting Lebanon, Abdalla died, leaving Nazha with eight children in what was at that time largely a man's world. Abdalla had instilled in his family an old Lebanese tradition, the importance of standing together. He had often said, "You can't break sticks that are bundled together, but piece by piece it is easy."

Nazha and the children ran the store, got jobs, and kept the family strong by working together.

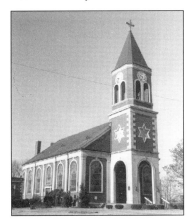

Many of Birmingham's Lebanese families resided on the city's Southside in close proximity to their churches, St. Elias Maronite Church at 836 8th St. South (above) and St. George's Melkite Greek-Catholic Church at 401 Tenth Ave. South (below).

Abdalla and Nazha Boohaker and their children in the 1920s.

Award-Winning Beauty

At its completion in 1925, the Alabama Power Company Building broke new ground for Southern architecture. Representing a refreshing departure from the "Chicago School" design, featured in most of the commercial skyscrapers in the Magic City, it was the city's first skyscraper to be finished on all four sides.

Authorities describe the power company building's style as "Neo-Gothic Art Moderne," but what made it different from its predecessors was the building's distinctive sculpture that became an integral part of its design. Statues were conceived not just as ornaments, but as metaphorical expressions of the services of the power company and as symbols of the corporate identity.

Three eight-foot figures above the entrance represent "Power, Light, and Heat." A golden statue of Electra holding sheaths of lightning bolts graces the top of the structure. In the 1920s, a time when electrical power service was being extended throughout Alabama, Electra represented the vitality of this "electrical progress."

Power company officials took great pride in the fact that most of the building materials—including

steel, brick, tile, pipe and lumber—came from within a 60-mile radius of Birmingham, but appreciation for the new building came from sources both near and far.

In 1929, the American Institute of Architects awarded the power company building its only gold medal and first prize for best commercial building at its Southern Architecture and Industrial Arts Exposition.

This limestone figure depictis "Light," a principal service of the power company.

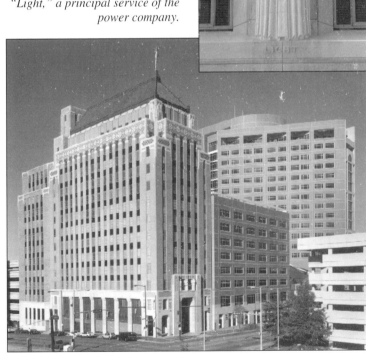

Today's Alabama Power Company Building, topped by the golden Electra, is flanked by a respectful new headquarters complex.

Palace for the Common Man

When the Alabama Theatre opened December 26, 1927, journalists touted it as a Christmas gift for Birmingham of unrivaled splendor. The one-and-a-half-million-dollar theatre lived up to its praise by giving ticketbuyers the chance to enter a luxurious fantasy for an evening of affordable entertainment.

The theatre's facade elaborately expressed the glamour, the illusion, and the mix of architectural styles which characterized the grand urban movie palaces of the 1920s, a period when moving pictures were at the height of fashion. Inside, 3,000 patrons were immersed in the lushness of Spanish and Moorish palaces.

In addition to the newsreels and silent films of the day, the Alabama presented stage entertainers direct from Broadway. A magnificent Wurlitzer organ installed on a moving elevator platform in the orchestra pit could imitate the human voice and every known musical instrument. The prices for the latest in entertainment ranged from 25 cents for a matinee to 60 cents for a nighttime show.

Today, the Alabama remains a "showplace of the South." A group of historic theatres and stores in the area, including Loveman's, the Lyric, and Carver Theatres, has recently been named the National Register Theatre & Retail District, and the target for revitalization efforts by the City of Birmingham.

Working to restore and manage the Alabama are these dedicated volunteers of Birmingham Landmarks, Inc.

True Tales
OF BIRMINGHAM

The People Behind TRUE TALES

For 60 weeks, this column profiled men and women from Birmingham's past who helped shape the city as we know it today. It also featured buildings and locations that still stand as testimony to the area's rich and diverse cultural heritage. This is the final TRUE TALES column, all 60 profiles of people and places appear in this book.

This column was made possible by: Larry Ragan, writing; Victor Hanson III, Tom Scarritt, concept; Gary Dobbs, Don Veasey and Birmingham Public Library Department of Archives and Manuscripts,

Pictured at Duncan House, Birmingham Historical Society's offices at Sloss Furnaces National Historic Landmark, are members of the TRUE TALES production staff. Front left to right: Ellen Davis, Kelly Cannon, Mary Frances Kihlstrom, Brenda Howell, and Marjorie White. Back left to right: Bill Jones, Philip Morris, Tom Scarritt, Larry Ragan, Scott Fuller, Joe Strickland, and Tim Abney.

photography; Ashlea Akins, Brenda Howell, and Bill Jones, research; Scott Fuller, design; Tim Abney, Amanda Adams, Kelly Cannon, Rhonda Covington, Ellen Davis, Mary Frances Kihlstrom, Tom Scarritt, Kay Henckell Smith, Joe Strickland, and Jim White, volunteer editors; Philip Morris, Time, Inc., *The Birmingham News*, and Birmingham Historical Society Publication Fund, John Holcomb III, Art Beattie, Victor Hanson III, financial support; Joe Bruno, Rochelle Gray, Nancy Wagnon, John Bragg, Betsy Hunter, Martin Hames, distribution; Marjorie White, editor/producer.

Index